Lots of things you want to know about GLADIATORS

...and some you don't!

Written and Illustrated by
David West

A⁺
Smart Apple Media

Published by Smart Apple Media, an imprint of Black Rabbit Books
P.O. Box 3263, Mankato, Minnesota 56002
www.smartapplemedia.com

Produced by David West ᛉ Children's Books
6 Princeton Court, 55 Felsham Road, London SW15 1AZ

Designed and illustrated by David West

Copyright © 2013 David West Children's Books

Library of Congress Cataloging-in-Publication Data

West, David, 1956-
Lots of things you want to know about gladiators : ... and some you don't! / David West.
pages cm. – (Lots of things you want to know about)
Includes index.
ISBN 978-1-62588-090-1
1. Gladiators–Rome–History–Juvenile literature. I. Title.
GV35.W47 2015
796.80937–dc23
2013030718
Printed in China
CPSIA compliance information DWCB15CP
311214

9 8 7 6 5 4 3 2 1

CONTENTS

Most Gladiators Were Slaves or Captured Enemy Soldiers

Rome's military success produced many captured enemy soldiers. They were sent to work in mines, sold as slaves, or bought for gladiator training.

There were also many free young men who gave up their freedom to enlist as gladiators.

Gladiators Trained at Special Schools

A gladiator was a trained fighter. He was owned by a master to whom he swore an oath. Gladiator school offered training, regular food, and a chance for fame and fortune.

Gladiators could keep their prize money and any gifts they received.

Gladiators Fought in Arenas Called Amphitheaters

Around 230 of these oval or circular arenas have been found throughout the Roman Empire. The largest of them is the Colosseum in Rome. It could seat 50,000 spectators.

Contests Had Two Referees

Most matches employed a senior referee and an assistant. They were equipped with long wooden staffs. They used these to caution or separate the gladiators during the match.

Some Gladiators Wore Armor

The heavily armored gladiators, called murmillos and secutors, carried a short sword called a gladius and a curved, rectangular shield called a scutum. They wore an arm guard called a manica, metal leg protectors called ocras, and a helmet.

Some Gladiators Used a Net

A net fighter was called a retiarius. They were armed with a three-pronged spear called a trident. The retiarius was lightly armored, wearing a manica and one or two ocras. The retiarius usually fought against the heavily-armed secutor.

He used the net to entangle his opponent before finishing him off with his trident.

Some Gladiators Fought on Horseback

Gladiators who fought on horseback were called equites. They started on horseback, but after they had thrown their lance, called a hasta, they dismounted and continued to fight on foot with their short sword.

Others Fought from Chariots

Those gladiators who fought from chariots were called essedariuses. Chariots were introduced to fights by **Julius Caesar** after the first century AD. He was impressed by the war chariots the ancient Britons used against his troops.

Some Gladiators Fought Lions

Gladiators called bestiarii fought wild animals such as lions, tigers, bears, and elephants in the arena. These mock hunts were held in the morning before the afternoon's main event of duels. Few animals survived, although they sometimes killed bestiarii.

A Defeated Gladiator Raised His Finger

In the earliest contests, death was the usual outcome of combat. Later, as the demand for gladiators began to exceed supply, a defeated gladiator might be spared. When a gladiator thought he was close to being killed, he raised his finger to stop the fight.

The Crowd Decided the Fate of a Defeated Gladiator

Once a gladiator had raised his finger, the referees would stop the fight. The man paying for the games, called the editor, would grant life or death, according to the spectators' wishes.

A Gladiator's Favorite Prize Was a Wooden Sword

The winner received a palm branch and a reward from the editor. A really good fighter might receive a laurel crown and money. The greatest reward was freedom, symbolized by the gift of a wooden sword.

Some Fights Ended in a Draw

Winning a fight without causing injury was praised. Several gladiators have been recorded as never injuring anyone in their entire careers. Matches ended in a draw when both gladiators gave up at the same time after a lengthy fight.

Gladiators Had Fans Like Modern-day Football Stars

Although they were of a lowly class in Roman society, the public idolized successful gladiators. Paintings of gladiators were displayed before the fights. If a rumor spread that gladiators were about to be exhibited, people flocked to the amphitheater for a view. A **senator**'s wife even secretly went to Egypt to marry a gladiator called Sergius.

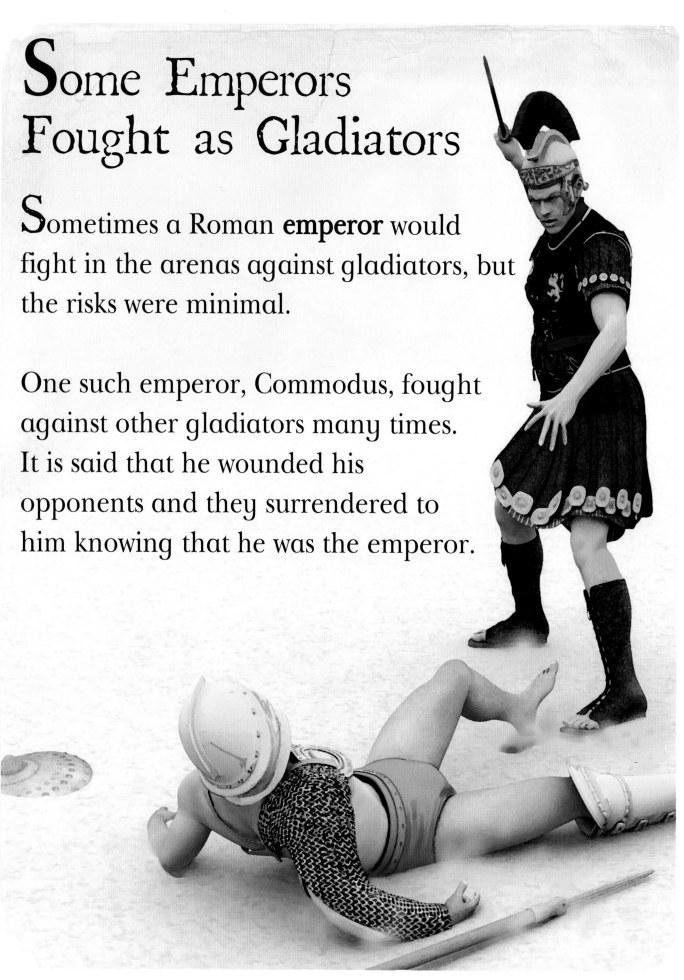

Some Emperors Fought as Gladiators

Sometimes a Roman **emperor** would fight in the arenas against gladiators, but the risks were minimal.

One such emperor, Commodus, fought against other gladiators many times. It is said that he wounded his opponents and they surrendered to him knowing that he was the emperor.

Gladiators Could Became Rich and Powerful

Some gladiators bought their freedom and retired in comfort. The emperor Tiberius offered several retired gladiators the equivalent of half a million dollars each to return to the arena. The general **Mark Antony** promoted gladiators to his personal guard.

The Gladiator Spartacus Led a Slave Rebellion

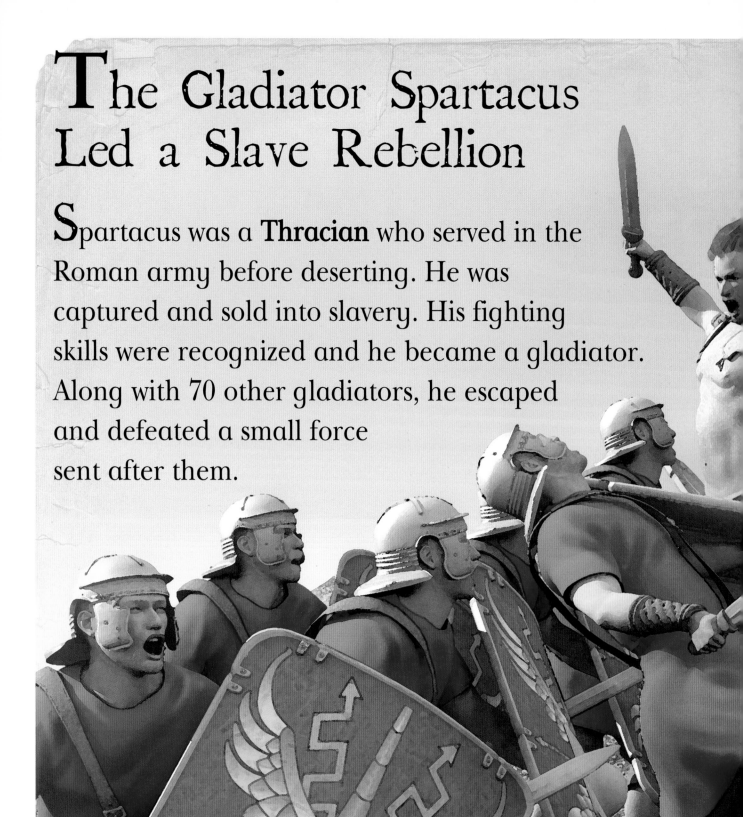

Spartacus was a **Thracian** who served in the Roman army before deserting. He was captured and sold into slavery. His fighting skills were recognized and he became a gladiator. Along with 70 other gladiators, he escaped and defeated a small force sent after them.

Over two years, 70,000 slaves flocked to his ranks. They defeated the Roman army several times before finally being defeated in 71 BC. Spartacus's body was never found.

Some Gladiators Were Women

Female gladiators called gladiatrixes started to appear in the arena around 60 AD. A marble relief from **Halicarnassus** shows two female gladiators named Amazon and Achillia. Their fight ended in a draw. Gladiatrixes may also have hunted boar and fought from chariots.

Glossary

emperor the ruler of an empire, in this case the Roman Empire

Halicarnassus an ancient Greek city in Turkey that was originally part of the Persian Empire and was captured by Alexander the Great before becoming part of the Roman Empire

Julius Caesar a famous general and ruler of Rome who conquered Gaul and was the first to invade Britain; he was eventually assassinated by a group of senators led by Marcus Brutus

Mark Antony a Roman politician and general who was a supporter and loyal friend of Julius Caesar

senator a member of a group of citizens who govern a country

Thracians a group of tribes living in central and southeastern Europe west of the Black Sea whom the Romans regarded as ferocious and bloodthirsty

Index